DATE DUE

SP 29 '95			
MR 30 '98			

DEMCO 38-296

STRAIGHT FROM THE HEART

José Jaramillo, accordionist, deceased, Albuquerque, N.M., 1984

Straight from the Heart

PORTRAITS OF TRADITIONAL HISPANIC MUSICIANS

Photographs by Jack Parsons

Essay by Jim Sagel

FOREWORD BY JACK LOEFFLER

UNIVERSITY OF NEW MEXICO PRESS

Albuquerque

Library of Congress Cataloging in Publication Data

Parsons, Jack, 1939–

 Straight from the heart : portraits of traditional Hispanic musicians /
photographs by Jack Parsons ; essay by Jim Sagel. — 1st ed.

  p. cm.

 ISBN 0-8263-1217-9 : $17.50

 1. Hispanic American musicians—Mexico—Portraits. 2. Folk
music—New Mexico—Pictorial works. I. Sagel, Jim. II. Title.

ML87.P3 1990

779'.978161680789—dc20

            90-35590
             CIP
             MN

For Becky, Mac, Chris, and Alex

CONTENTS

vii

ACKNOWLEDGMENTS

I OWE A huge debt of gratitude to my close friends Jack and Katherine Loeffler who made this book possible. Their years of dedicated field work, collecting the old songs of the musicians in this book, and those of many, many others, made my work easy. Their gift of this music to the people of New Mexico through recordings, folk festivals, books, and radio programs will endure as a major cultural contribution.

Thanks are also due to the National Endowment for the Arts Folk Arts Program, the New Mexico Arts Division, the Santa Fe Council for the Arts, and the Folk Art Foundation of the Museum of New Mexico for their generous support of a whole range of Hispanic music projects with which I've been involved over the past six years and which allowed me to make the photographs for this book.

I am also indebted to Suzanne Jamison, Cipriano Vigil, Enrique Lamadrid, and again Jack Loeffler for my good fortune in being involved with the Entriega Project, the most comprehensive survey to date of this genre of folk music. This project enabled me to take many of the photographs in this book, and the wide-ranging talents and companionship of the participants made this long-term survey seem all too short.

Thanks also to Jim Sagel, writer and friend, Ray Belcher and Sheila Satkowski, and Beth Hadas and the staff at UNM Press whose professionalism and humor made the hard work of book production enjoyable.

And, most of all, my deepest appreciation to all those musicians who allowed me into their lives. I wish they could all be in this book, but the limitations of space make this impossible. Deletions were made as a result of my own inadequacies as a photographer and not because of theirs as musicians.

Jack Parsons
Santa Fe, 1990

Quien canta, sus males espanta.

HE WHO SINGS CHASES THE BLUES AWAY.

FOREWORD

Jack Loeffler

FOR FOUR CENTURIES, the mountains of northern New Mexico have rung with echoes of music sung and played by people whose spoken language is Spanish. The first Spanish colonists emigrated northward along the Rio Grande del Norte and settled on land which Pueblo Indians and their ancestors had trod for millennia. The Spaniards remained isolated from their European homeland and even their Spanish neighbors to the south for years on end. They evolved a culture of their own.

Mestizaje was inevitable, and this "mixture" of Spanish and Indian resulted in a new race. Even though their cultures remained distinct, certain characteristics became fundamental to everyone, including a prevailing sense of the sustaining earth.

Within Hispanic culture, a whole system of folklore and folk music developed through which the evolving tradition was passed from one generation to the next. Musical forms, narrative ballads, and poetry flowered within a single generation and then faded from living memory. Still, the musical heritage of the Hispanic Rio Grande del Norte is rich with melody and poetry although it has rarely caught the attention of mainstream America.

The decades following World War II have seen a great change in traditional cultures throughout North America. Of the myriad factors which have hastened the pace of change, the two most predominant are the accessibility of transportation and the omnipresence of the media. Ethnicity has become an endangered characteristic of our species. Points of view which have served humanity well for thousands of years are being displaced by a seemingly universal attention on materialism, resulting in a frenetic restlessness and lack of spiritual satisfaction. Individual and cultural identity become nebulous.

In the early 1960s, I began to delight in listening to the sounds generated by traditional cultures. My quest has taken me throughout the American Southwest, Mexico and beyond, and has resulted in personal enrichment that is inexpressible. In the mid-1970s, my wife, Katherine, and I began to record the traditional music of the Hispanic Rio Grande del Norte for a multifaceted folklore project entitled La Música de los Viejitos, which has resulted in the field collecting of some 3,300 recordings of folksongs for posterity and presentation. In 1982, my close friend Jack Parsons and I collaborated on a documentary film concerning Hispanic folk music in New Mexico and southern Colorado. Subsequently, we traveled to the homes of all the musicians still living whose music we had recorded. Jack photographed these musicians whose lives frequently reflect their long tradition and whose music portrays a culture which continues to prevail and evolve.

Many of those photographs are presented in this publication, which stands as a body of work whose worth as a cultural document is inestimable. The heart of Hispanic culture is visible herein, and we all look to Jack Parsons with gratitude for committing his talent and considerable energy to presenting this collection of portraits.

Jack Loeffler
SANTA FE, NEW MEXICO
1990

STRAIGHT FROM THE HEART

PASIÓN Y TRADICIÓN: LOS MÚSICOS DEL PUEBLO

Jim Sagel

The sun has long since melted behind el Cerro Pedernal. The breath of a breeze stirs through the peach trees, wafting the scent of freshly cut alfalfa through the portal where the man sits, his long day of work done, dinner eaten, cigarette glowing in the satisfied darkness. Thick hands, burnished by plow handle and rope, grasp a guitar missing the D-string and pluck out the tune armies of heartsick soldiers marched to during the Mexican Revolution.

The newly married novios, bleary-eyed from emotion and too much champagne, sit in the balloon-draped Knights of Columbus Hall, surrounded by family and padrinos, while the gravel throated singer in the black dress sings "la entriega de los novios."

Adán se quedó dormido
En un hermoso vergel—
Ya no hay padre, ya no hay madre—
Ahora lo que hay es mujer.

Adam fell asleep
In the beautiful garden of life—
There is no more father, there is no more mother—
Now what you have is a wife.

Bent-backed and wizened, his surprisingly nimble fingers still dance over the strings of his century-old violin as he plays "la Varsoviana," even though the majority of his audience at the local senior citizens center can only tap their heavy toes and remember a time when they could "put their little foot right there."

The family conjunto—two brothers, a tío, and his dark-eyed daughter—belt out an electrified version of "el corrido de Rosita Alvírez," a turn-of-the-century ballad recounting the tragic tale of a young woman who attends a dance without her mother's permission, an appropriate enough choice of songs in this dancehall where legend has it another muchachita bonita defied her mother, going to a fandango during Lent and ending up waltzing in the arms of a handsome stranger whose wingtips suddenly changed into cloven hooves.

Lubbock and Long Beach tourists nod approvingly between mouthfuls of honey-drenched sopaipillas as her delicate fingers assault the guitar strings, evoking the pain of la Llorona in this most pleasant of places. "Hay muertos que no hacen ruido, Llorona, y es más grande su penar," she sings—"There are dead souls that make no sound, Llorona, but their pain is so much more."

The ranchero, carpintero, santero, and penitente hermano, who is actually a poet, irrigates his chile and calabazas in the moonlight and sings alabados to the stars, head thrown back, stringing the words of his ancestors on a melodic thread haunting and mournful, startling the neighbors in the canyon below and scandalizing their dogs.

These are the musicians of the mountain villages, the river valleys, the llanos, the trailer courts, and the desert. Son los músicos del pueblo—the musicians of the people.

The word *pueblo,* of course, denotes a place as well as a people, and that duality of meaning is no linguistic coincidence. In the Hispanic view, the place where the people dwell is the people, and the people are the place. Nowhere is this identification more potent than in Nuevo México and Viejo Colorado (as I refer to the Hispanic southern part of the state whose lower boundary arbitrarily separates a common people). Nowhere has the landscape played a more crucial role in determining history and shaping the culture of a people.

At once forbidding and nurturing, this rugged land isolated the early Hispanic settlers from their "civilization," even while it provided all the resources necessary to create a more austere, natural way of life. Learning from the people they called the Pueblos, the Spanish pobladores developed a culture rooted in "la tierra," a society whose lifeblood was the precious water that flowed through the arteries of the acequias, the ditches that sustained the cycle of life.

Though some of those acequias are lined with concrete now and still others are choked with dust, the land continues to be the center of the life of the pueblo. It is what motivates the electrical engineer to return home from Dallas and hook up a double-wide mobile home next to his abuelita's crumbling adobe. It is what causes the disillusioned dancer to leave her husband and the ballet company in order to grow apples and garlic on a generational farm miles from any paved road.

Here, the land still spurs gun battles and barroom ballads. "¡Tierra o Muerte!" declare the hand-lettered billboards that sprout from the soil of stolen land grants. Here, the land is at the core of every dream and the only thing still worth dying for.

Thus, it was more than simply "desirable" that Jack Parsons photograph this group of musicians in their natural environment; it was necessary if he was to capture their real faces, their true selves.

And capture them he has. Here are "los músicos" in the places where they live and work, in the places that define them, pausing for a photograph in front of owner-built lumbermills in the heart of the sierra, beside Ford Fairlanes parked in the projects, on couches under velvet paintings of the Last Supper flanked by family photos of graduating daughters and sad-eyed sons in military uniforms.

6

The shovel that Floyd Trujillo holds in his hand probably says more about him than the harmonica he plays so skillfully; it may even say more about his music. Certainly, had Jack Parsons asked the Abiquíu musician and penitente to come in to the studio to be photographed, the resultant image would have been out of context, stultified, and somehow unreal. It would not have been unlike listening to a recording of a wedding marcha while seated at a desk in a university classroom. You might learn something about the music—the melody line, tempo, and instrumentation—but you'd hardly understand what it's like to be in a wedding march, tripping drunkenly under the heaving human bridge of interlocked arms—shouting, sweating, laughter pulsating in your brain, tío Fernando whistling through his three good teeth, bestowing a playful blessing on the head of every sobrino ducking by and a less innocent pat a little lower on the anatomy of all the nephews' novias.

These photographs capture, as well as a camera possibly can, the real "marcha." We see the music in the eyes of each musician; we can almost read the history etched in their faces like rivulets in an adobe wall. Naturally, many of the actual adobe walls that surround these músicos have been hidden by dark sheets of walnut paneling, but San José and San Antonio still stand guard over the VCR. And these violinists and accordion players posing next to their long-suffering GMC's and Chevy trocas beam the same proud smile their grandfathers once reserved for their finest mares. Some, of course, still have their own horses growing fat and useless in the corral out behind the chante. Though they may never use that aging Morgan now that they've sold off their National Forest permisos and all but three head of their cattle, they stubbornly keep him, for you never know when you might need a horse. Which is why there is such a wonderful clutter in the homes and yards of these musicians: they were taught by their parents who were taught by their parents' parents never to·waste anything, never to throw anything away—be it food, materials, or the songs of their ancestors.

That's a frontier value, a lesson learned in the blood and passed down through the generations in the dichos and versos, the costumbres and creencias—all the traditions that make up the collective wisdom of the culture. Life was hard in this remote frontier; it still is today. It's that isolation that bred and continues to breed a people who take tremendous pride in their past and in their enduring ability to prosper in the secluded corners of this beautiful land.

Hard work and self-reliance are at the core of this culture. Here, people have always had to rely on their own wits and strength to construct a life using only what the earth could provide. Resourceful as an individual might be, however, he could never survive on his own. It took a communal effort to dig the ditches that would channel the scarce river water to the fields; it took cooperation to produce an abundant harvest and to build the church in which to thank the God who had made all that bounty possible.

Thus, a strong sense of community developed in the soul of la gente. It started in the family, the center of a circle that included not only parents and children but also grand-parents, great-grandparents, uncles, aunts, and cousins. That circle was widened by the tradition of compadrazgo as a network of padrinos and compadres tied the extended families together. All the interrelated families and neigh-bors, in turn, were united in the spiritual sphere, la comu-nidad de fe. It was this community of faith that gave iden-tity to the people and sustained them in the inevitable times of pain and deprivation. And it was respect that provided the necessary bond to hold all these circles together—respect for one's parents, for one's elders, for one's church, and for the traditions of the past.

For all its strictness, however, this "respeto" has never worn a stern face. Passion has always been at the heart of the Hispanic tradition—un gusto por la vida, a flat-out joy in the simple act of living. This gusto finds its expression in an unsurpassed tradition of humor: few cultures laugh more heartily or more often. No doubt tempered by the harshness of daily existence—in the end, what can you do in the face of drought and disease but laugh?—this Hispanic sense of humor even makes light of death. In the storytelling tradi-tion, la comadre Sebastiana, the walking, talking bony per-sonification of death, is often the subject of practical jokes and downright derision (though she, of course, always wins in the end). But it is this ability to laugh in the face of death, this intimate and personal relation with one's own mortality that pumps up the lungs and produces those irrepressible shouts of joy—¡los gritos de alegría!

Pasión y tradición. You see it reflected in each of these faces—a reverence for tradition and a passion for life. Yet, there is no conformity in these expressions: los músicos are the exceptions, not the rule. They come from every walk of life and they live in every possible location nuevomexicanos and viejocoloradianos can live, from Alamosa to Tularosa, from the silent cliffs of Canjilón to the bustling barrios of Martíneztown and Barelas.

And they approach their music in as many different ways. Some are "muy quemados," as they say—well-oiled professionals who do regular weekend gigs at the Holiday Inn. Others have never used a microphone nor heard themselves recorded; they play principally for themselves, an occasional family reunion, or perhaps the choir at the 10:30 mass on Sunday mornings. There are postmasters here, retired railroad workers, teachers, and technicians. There are migrant laborers, men and women who have spent most of their lives piscando papas and thinning beets under the relentless sun. Here, too, are those who went for years without seeing the sun, working under the earth in the coal mines of Walsenburg and Ludlow. There are those who made the long annual trek "en la borrega," following the great sheep herds as far away as Utah and Wyoming, and there are those who continue commuting up a different kind of "hill," working in the Los Alamos National Laboratory or guarding their secretive gates.

Many of these traditional musicians still eke out a living in the most traditional way, on the land. Against all odds, they hold onto their land, still planting even when there is no profit in it, still running their reduced herds of cattle at a certain loss. Naturally, they complain about how their life isn't like it used to be "en los tiempos de antes," back in the days when the land was free and open—before Thomas Catron and his pack of abogados ladrones came to gobble up the land grants, before "el Oso Esmokey" lumbered on the scene with his cattleguards and barbed wire, before the Army Corps of Engineers dammed up the water for Albuquerque golf courses, before that second "army" of assessors arrived to tax many of the subsistence ranchers off their land. "Todo está cambiado," these músicos will tell you, and they are right. Everything has changed—everything, that is, except for their own spirit, that rare and beautiful stubbornness that keeps them clinging to the old ways and singing the old songs.

There's a wonderful paradox in all of this: these músicos who do so much to preserve the heritage of their people through song have always been among the most nonconformist individuals in Hispanic society. On a personal level, their lives often seem to contradict many of the traditional values. They don't follow the rules: when they should have been out in the garden escardando el chile, they were sitting in the shade of the portal instead, fiddling with a violin while the hoe lay idle on the step. They were the disobedient rebels, ignoring their mothers who warned them that the life of a musician was scarcely a cut above that of a drunk. It was true, of course, that a number of the local músicos tended to be rather legendary borrachos, but they had their place in the social order too.

It's all a matter of balance. One must work hard and be obedient in order to survive; one must sing and dance de vez en cuando—tirar chancla once in a while—in order to live. Thus, the figure of the pícaro who provides balance and perspective to the industrious cristiano who's all sweat and prayers and no play. Like his Indian primo Coyote, the pícaro dwells on the fringes of society, constantly poking fun at its limitations and excesses. They call him lazy, but that's only because he refuses to work for anyone else, having never developed what he considers an unhealthy respect for authority. He never fits in nor does he ever care to. In fact, he's quite carefree, doing just what he pleases, thumbing his nose at convention, acting perfectly outrageous and getting away with it because when his vecinos aren't too afraid to ask him to stop, they're begging him to go on, for his independence is as entertaining as it is enticing. He's a great storyteller, having honed his wit to get by. He loves to overindulge in drink, food, or whatever is available for the indulging, and he usually plays one or more musical instruments exceedingly well, often at the same time. He's a one-man band, in fact—the one who can play "con seis sentidos a la vez—with six senses at once," as músico and santero Max Trujillo of Taos puts it, referring to the usual five senses and that special sixth sentido he defines by simply pointing to his head. In the end, the pícaro is crazy in a meaningful way and meaningful in a crazy way: he's so far out he's the only one who can see how it all fits together.

Not every face in this volume belongs to a pícaro, of course, but there is an edge of daring in many of the smiles, an air of pure fun in the eyes. Even some of the most eroded faces here have the look of a child who has not yet learned that laughter is often mistaken for a sign of disrespect. One can almost hear a wicked riff sounding from the guitar, a saucy verse coming from those lips in the finest picaresque tradition of insulting your host and getting paid for it. Here is the pícaro-músico going from house to house on New Year's Day, dando los días—creating humorous verses right on the spot that rhyme around the dueño's name, usually in a less than flattering way. But it's all done with good humor and high spirits, and the spirits fly even higher as the morning progresses and the músico and his inebriated band of compañeros take their pay en tragos de juisque.

This tradition of spontaneous versification reached its height of expression in "el valse chiquiado," a special pieza popular at the old fandangos. Though the dance itself has nearly died out with the passing of the ancianos, many of the versos still survive. When the bastonero, or caller of the dances, would announce "el valse chiquiado," everyone knew the fun was about to begin for tradition dictated that the male first sing a verse to his intended partner before taking her out to dance. She, in turn, had to "echarle un verso también," upping the ante and multipying the mirth of the listeners, for most of the verses were delightfully sarcastic. The hombre might woo his prospective partner like this:

Viene la luna saliendo
Vestida de seda negra—
Anda dile a tu mamá
Si quiere ser mi suegra.

The moon is rising
Dressed in black silk—
Go and ask your mother
If she'd like to be my mother-in-law.

To which the mujer would reply:

Viene la luna saliendo
Vestida de seda colorada—
Anda dile a tu mamá
Que no te quiero pa'nada.

The moon is rising
Dressed in red silk—
Go and tell your mama
That I don't want you at all.

Sometimes the pícaro would pick on an entire community like the legendary poeta and borracho José María Martínez did when he made up a verso about the people of Cañones:

Si el Cerro de Pedernal
Se volviera chicharrones—

Todavía no se acabalaran
Los cuscos de Cañones.

Even if Pedernal Peak
Turned into chicharrones—
There still wouldn't be enough
For the greedy folks of Cañones.

Though there are, no doubt, some prodigious appetites for chicharrones up that way, the verso doesn't really single out the pueblito of Cañones; don José María surely cooked up some choice couplets for the people of Coyote as well, not to mention Abiquíu, Río Puerco, Gallina, Arroyo de Agua, and any other place he may have wandered. And though you might have been able to hide in some of those chiseled red canyons, there was no escaping the pícaro at social functions and bailes. Even at wedding dances he was there with sharp tongue and quick wit, ready to immortalize your faults and foibles with a verso atinado. The following verse, for instance, not only has long outlived Samuel Madril's prolonged state of bachelorhood, but the poor pock-faced soltero himself:

Pasó el mes de marzo
Pasó el mes de abril—
Ya le dieron calabazas
A don Samuel Madril.

The month of March has gone by
The month of April too—
When Samuel Madril asked, "Do you want to get
   married?"
They answered, "Not with you."

¡Qué falta de respeto!—a terrible lack of respect—and
all the more reason to laugh in a culture so preóccupied
with propriety and decorum. After all, if it weren't for the
músicos, the Samuel Madriles of the world would take
themselves too seriously, and the rest of us might trick ourselves into believing we never could end up in his lonely
shoes. Yet, it's more than that, as the above verso reveals.
The line, "Ya le dieron calabazas a don Samuel Madril"—
literally, "They gave pumpkins to Mr. Samuel Madril," is a
reference to an old Hispanic custom associated with mar-
riage. When a suitor proposed to a woman, he received either a formal acceptance (usually communicated from the
parents of the novia to the parents of the novio), or he
awoke one morning to find a pumpkin in front of his door,
which meant, of course, that his proposal had been rebuffed.
This verso, then, does more than simply make light of don
Samuel Madril; it also celebrates a cultural custom, just as
"el verso chiquiado" preserves the memory of a traditional
dance that in its mating of formality and fun expresses the
unique character of Hispanic culture as it evolved in the
northern frontier.

   And so, it is this band of nonconformists—these músicos—who are in an ironic sense the keepers of tradition.

The music they create on their two-button accordions and battered mandolins informs the soul while it lightens the heart, for these piezas and canciones are not solely musical forms, but vessels of culture as well. From the polkas to the alabados, the wide-ranging repertoire of los músicos del pueblo expresses the secular and religious traditions of the people who have made this land their home for four centuries.

How many generations have danced "el valse de la escoba," three-stepping with a broom in adobe salas illuminated by the flickering light of arañas, hand-hewn chandeliers dripping with tallow candles? What nameless ancestors cradled the uncertain future in their calloused hands, swaying together to the tune of "la cuna" on mud-packed suelos strewn with straw? "El cutilio," "el chotis," "la camila," "la cuadrilla"—all the wonderful old piezas conjure up a time of ceremonious festivity, and though those who know how to perform the intricate dance steps are rapidly disappearing, the music perpetuates the spirit of the past.

The history of the pueblo is also sung in dozens of distinct forms, many of which are hundreds of years old. One of the oldest forms, the "romance," ultimately can be traced back to its roots in the epic poetry of medieval Spain. The early romances which began to develop in the thirteenth century were ballads loosely based on the old epics, narrating the exploits of noblemen and soldiers. By the sixteenth century, a rich tradition of historical, religious, novelesque, and burlesque ballads was in full flower in Spain. Many of these romances were transmitted to the New World and have remained remarkably unchanged to the present day. Edwin Berry of Tomé, New Mexico, a living compendium of traditional folk music, sings a version of "el romance del Señor don Gato," a humorous ballad from sixteenth-century Spain. The narrative begins with the line: "Estaba el señor don Gato, en silla de oro sentado—Mr. Cat was sitting on the seat of a golden chair." As the ballad progresses, the elegantly dressed feline learns that a bride has been located for him. In his excitement, he jumps from the chair, smashes his head, and dies. The romance concludes with the mice rejoicing in a huge celebration.

A related, and more recent form, is the corrido, a type of ballad that originated as a means of commemorating and communicating great or catastrophic events. Like the romance, the corrido also relates the adventures of heroes; however, unlike its antecedent, the corrido does not focus on nobility but, rather, on such "uncommon" common men as the Mexican revolutionary Pancho Villa. Though the majority of the corridos sung today originated in Mexico, there are many of local origin as well, and the tradition continues to thrive among los músicos nuevomexicanos y viejocoloradianos. The Tierra Amarilla Courthouse Raid of 1967, for example, inspired a number of traditional corridos about Reíes López Tixerina. And though the national networks provided exhaustive coverage of the 1980 New Mexico State Prison riot, Al Hurricane, Jr., narrated the tragic story in the old way with his "Corrido de la prisión."

The décima, a song composed of a series of ten-line stanzas, is another ancient form being kept alive by these contemporary troubadors, as is the relación. One such relación aglutinante—literally, "stuck-together narrative" or list song—is "La rana," the humorous story of a very noisy frog. As sung by Alamosa musician Salomón Chávez, the relación begins:

Estaba la rana cantando debajo del agua—
Cuando la rana salió a cantar
Vino la mosca y le hizo callar.
La mosca la rana,
La rana que estaba sentada
Cantando debajo del agua.

The frog was singing under the water—
When the frog came out to sing
The fly arrived and made him shut up.
The fly the frog,
The frog that was sitting
Under the water singing.

A new character emerges in each succeeding verse to force the previous singer to "shut his mouth." By the end of the song, the singer must draw a considerable breath, for the list he sings is ridiculously long:

Cuando el hombre salió a cantar
Vino la suegra y le hizo callar.

La suegra el hombre,
El hombre el perro,
El perro el gato,
El gato la rata,
La rata la escoba,
La escoba la araña,
La araña la mosca,
La mosca la rana,
La rana que estaba sentada
Debajo del agua cantando.

When the man came out to sing
The mother-in-law came and made him shut up.
The mother-in-law the man,
The man the dog,
The dog the cat,
The cat the rat,
The rat the broom,
The broom the spider,
The spider the fly,
The fly the frog,
The frog that was sitting
Under the water singing.

The relación ends on an appropriately satiric note:

Cuando la suegra salió a cantar
Ni el mismo diablo le hizo callar.

When the mother-in-law came out to sing
Not even the devil himself could make her shut up!

There is a strong strain of suegra-baiting in Hispanic tradition, ranging from the dicho, "Las suegras ni de azúcar son buenas—Mothers-in-law are awful even if they're made out of sugar," to the verse tacked onto the traditional ranchera, "Allá en el Rancho Grande":

Cuando se muera mi suegra
Que la entierren boca abajo—
Para si quiere salir
Que se vaya más pa'bajo.

When my mother-in-law dies
Bury her face down—
So if she tries to get out
She'll just keep going down.

One can readily understand how the need for such musical "escape valves" would arise in such a closely knit society made up of extended families often sharing rambling, interconnected homes. But there were other means of escape as well, most notably the tradition of juegos, or games. Here, too, music played an important role, especially in the widely popular game known as "el juego de los cañutes." A sort of shell game, los cañutes called on a player to hide an object inside one of four cañutes—pipes or tubes. Each cañute had a name: el uno, el dos, el mulato, and el cinchado (the "cinched" one, i.e., a pipe with a string or rag tied around it). It fell to the opponent to guess which cañute held the "escondijo." If he was successful, he would win the cañutes and the chance to sing a "cañutero," that is, a verse of victory.

Naturally, music was involved with work as well as play in songs about "la borrega" and "la pisca"—the long migrations north to herd sheep and harvest vegetables. And, of course, there is the ongoing tradition of las mañanitas, those lovely songs sung in the early dawn outside the window of a sleepy neighbor on his or her birthday.

> *El día en que tú naciste*
> *Nacieron todas las flores—*
> *Y en la pila del bautismo*
> *Cantaron los ruiseñores.*

> *Your birthday was the day*
> *When all the flowers were born—*
> *And at the baptismal font*
> *Nightingales sang their song.*

Here, as in so many cases, the music is inseparable from the tradition. There could be no "mañanitas" without a guitarra and a shivering chorus of vecinos y parientes singing the words of the melody they've all known since their juventud: "¡Qué linda está la mañana en que vengo a saludarte!"

Yet another musical form which embodies an important cultural tradition is the indita. While the romance and the décima are rooted in the distant European past, the indita reflects the mestizaje which characterizes the culture of the Americas. From the moment they set spurred foot in the fertile soil of this northerly land, los españoles have been in continuous contact with its indigenous inhabitants. Though the history of the four-hundred-year relationship between the Pueblos and the Spanish has not always been a gentle one, the two great cultures are inextricably linked through blood and custom. That association finds expression in las inditas, a series of unique songs that reflect an Indian influence in the melody line and subject matter; the dance steps that accompany the music similarly reveal a stylized imitation of Pueblo dances.

While Indian culture has had a profound influence on Hispanic life-style, it is perhaps religion which most permeates and colors the daily existence of the nuevomexicano and viejocoloradiano. Religion here means more than mass on Sunday. That army of santos in your mother's bedroom is on duty seven days a week, as the Santo Niño de Atocha is called upon every night to watch over an errant child, and San Antonio is pressed into service several times a day to locate missing keys, rings, and eyeglasses. San Judas, of course, must not be bothered too often as he is the saint of last resort, but he is there when he is needed, working miracles in the ICU when even the doctors have lost hope.

Here the sign of the cross is as prevalent as a handshake, whether it's to ward off a dustdevil or to initiate the prayer before dinner—whether it's to fend off the evil eye of the resident bruja or to bless a daughter before she departs to college. God is palpable, real—wrapped up in the language itself. "Buenos días le dé Dios—May God grant you a good day" is the greeting that begins the day, and when the nuevomexicano or viejocoloradiano speaks of his plans for the following morning, he ends with the inevitable postscript, "God willing—Dios sirviendo."

Thus, it is no surprise that we find countless intersections between the secular and religious traditions in the music. Many of the músicos themselves sing "la entriega de los novios" in one breath and a raunchy corrido about that mujerero Gabino Barrera in the next. And even those who don't know the name of the local priest possess an inherent respect for the religion of their antepasados. The late Alfredo Vigil of Chimayó, for instance, used to claim that no disbeliever could play his violin because he had written the names of the Holy Trinity on a scrap of paper which he had slipped inside the antique instrument. Once, he said, a músico from a nearby village tried to play the violin, but all he could produce was a chorus of screeching groans.

Just as that apparently atheistic musician revealed the state of his soul in the squawking of the violin, the penitente pitero expresses the depth of his belief in the haunting tones of the flute that accompany the Holy Week processions. Nowhere has the tradition of Hispanic religious music been more highly evolved and preserved than in the alabados,

24

those long, brooding chants which seem to wring grief out of the ears. Over the centuries of isolation in the northern frontier, the members of the hermandades kept their spiritual traditions alive in the rituals, prayers, and songs they religiously passed down from generation to generation.

Ven, pecador y verás
A Jesús Sacramentado
Padeciendo por el hombre,
Tan cruelmente azotado.

Come, sinner, and you will see
Christ of the Sacrament,
Suffering for mankind,
Cruelly scourged by the whip.

Thus begins the first of 164 verses of an alabado recorded from a penitente libro de rezos. Of course, the tradition of self-flagellation was one of the things that set Jean Baptiste Lamy and subsequent archbishops against the penitentes, but whatever physical excesses existed were largely exaggerated and manipulated as an excuse for intolerance. The ironic fact of the matter is that, had it not been for those solitary moradas scattered in the remote mountain villages, the church itself might not have survived in this region—and we surely would have lost one of the rarest and most beautiful musical traditions of the Southwest.

An equally unique tradition is that of the folk drama. On

Good Friday, the penitente hermanos have traditionally re-enacted the Passion of Christ, though the dramatization has become more ritualized in recent years. Other ancient folk plays, such as "los Pastores," can ultimately be traced back to the medieval morality plays. Like those didactic dramas of a millennium ago, "los Pastores" calls upon the audience to respond actively to the shepherds and other characters of the play. Niños and ancianos alike boo the redfaced Lucifer, cheer the sword-wielding San Miguel el Arcángel when he wrestles the serpent to the floor, and laugh at Bartolo, el gran huevón, the lazy "everyman" who resists leaving the comfort of his bedroll even to witness the birth of the King of Kings.

"Las Posadas," another Christmas folk drama, requires the actual participation of the pueblo, as a group representing Joseph and Mary sings at the door of a home and another group within responds with verses that express reluctance at opening that door.

"Posada te pide, amado casero, por sólo una noche, la Reina del Cielo—The Queen of Heaven, good neighbor, asks shelter in your home for just one night," sing the freezing peregrinos.

"Pues, si es una reina quien lo solicita, ¿cómo es que de noche anda tan solita?" question the singers from within— "Well, if it's really a queen that's asking to come in, why is she all alone in the middle of the night?"

At last, the musical appeal to the collective conscience is successful and the door is opened, as man and God are reunited over a steaming cup of chocolate and a plate of bizcochitos.

The sublime and the vulgar come together, too, in "los Matachines," a mysterious pageant that also unites the Spanish and Indian cultures. Related to "los Moros y Cristianos," the ancient horseback dramatization of the expulsion of the Moors from Spain still enacted in the Hispanic North today, "los Matachines" has been transformed by contact with indigenous culture—it is, in fact, performed by both Hispanic and Indian groups. In the New World, the Spanish Monarca has become the Aztec emperor Moctezuma, and the figure of the young girl dressed in white to symbolize the power of good is known as la Malinche in honor of Hernán Cortez's Indian interpreter and mother of the hemisphere's first mestizo.

The masked matachines with their bejeweled headdresses and three-pronged scepters dance their highly ritualized steps while the wild man, el abuelo, whirls aimlessly on the perimeter of the group and at the outer limits of socially acceptable behavior, scandalizing and delighting the crowd of spectators who wait in anticipation for the climax of the drama when the force of evil, represented by the torito, is symbolically shot and castrated by the whooping abuelo. Unlike the other ancient juegos dramáticos, there is no spoken dialogue in "los Matachines." Like a Pueblo dance, the meaning is conveyed by the movement of the dancers and the mesmerizing tones of the music.

One who has played for "los Matachines" is Dr. Roberto

Vialpando of Alcalde, New Mexico, just north of the ancient pueblo site of Yunge-Oweenge, where don Juan de Oñate established that first capital of San Gabriel some four centuries ago. One of the first native norteños to earn a college degree, Dr. Vialpando describes himself as having been "born to be a musician," yet it wasn't until he was well into the seventh decade of his life that he picked up a violin and taught himself to play. When Dr. Vialpando was a child, his father refused to allow him to learn how to play the instrument. "He thought music was 'pura parranda,'" Dr. Vialpando remembers. "There were two things he wouldn't permit me to be—ni abogado ni músico—neither a lawyer nor a musician."

Though the young Vialpando obeyed his family's wishes, avoiding that pair of unscrupulous professions, he never lost his love for la música. And in spite of the fact that parents warned their children about the evils of the guitar, there was and continues to be a tradition of affection and respect for the village musician. Like the mayordomo of the acequia, the leader of the altar society, and the hermano mayor of the penitentes, the músico is highly valued in Hispanic society. For without that guitarrista, cantadora, and violinista, the voices of the past might lapse into silence.

His first guitar was an empty sardine can strung with wire. Pablo Trujillo, guitarist for Los Alegres de Taos, didn't sit around as a niño waiting for his parents to buy him a lira. He made his own (even though it created a terrible racket—"un ruido muy feo," as he recalls). And, like the vast majority of the other músicos pictured in this volume, don Pablo never had a music teacher.

In the view of the majority culture of the United States, the adjective *self-taught* connotes amateurism; here in Nuevo México y Viejo Colorado, teaching oneself how to do anything, whether it's to play the accordion or to position twenty-five-foot pine vigas on the roof of a house, is more than a virtue—it's a way of life. The value of self-sufficiency, so inbred over the centuries, continues to be a necessary skill for survival in this society, which remains as isolated as always, though that isolation is now more economic than geographic. Yet, we seem to prefer it that way—we need our space, we prize our freedom. We insist on doing things our own way.

That's why my father-in-law steadfastly refuses to take a tire into the shop for repair, even at his eighty-four years of age: why should he "tirar diez pesos dioquis" to pay someone for something he can very well do himself, even though he may spend the entire afternoon pounding at the stubborn rim with a sledgehammer and patching the terminal tube in ten different places. It's the same tradition of relying on oneself that motivated that viejo from up north to take his medical problems into his own hands. Just released from the hospital after prostate surgery, he went to a baile and danced until he literally collapsed. After arriving home and realizing he was passing blood in his urine, he went to his garage to dig out the battery syringe that reminded him of the instrument his urologist had used in the hospital.

After washing the acid from the syringe, he proceeded to flush out his own bladder using liberal amounts of plain tap water.

Though that example may be a bit extreme, it is completely true and not altogether atypical in this land of self-reliance where three-quarters of life's problems can be solved with a pair of pliers, a length of baling wire, and a willingness to "quebrar la cabeza"—literally, "break one's head," i.e., to figure something out. Here, a man's livelihood once depended upon his ability to train a horse; thus it's only natural he would now learn how to tear down and rebuild an engine. Here, my wife's great-grandmother once painstakingly unraveled her empty tobacco pouches, saving even the delicate thread in order to resew the material back into dishtowels, so it's no surprise the bisnieta she never knew would make a life out of spinning thread and weaving.

And so, we have the self-taught musician, the mandolinist who picked up a dusty family heirloom at the flea market and began fooling around with it until she had learned how to play, much in the same way one first learns how to speak, by imitation—through trial and error. The analogy is not casual, for the learning of a native tongue is not simply the acquisition of vocabulary: along with the words, one learns a way of perceiving the world, a cultural context which is part and parcel of the linguistic system. Likewise, the músico absorbs the cultural heritage inherent in the old piezas and romances he learns how to play, and thus the tradition is passed on in a way no formal teacher could accomplish.

Naturally, there are those who did have a teacher, most often that man sitting at the head of the dinner table. In the Española valley, for example, the name Serrano has become synonymous with music, as the elder brothers, don Tranquilino and don Juan, who have been músicos for well over half a century, have passed their talent down to an ever-widening circle of hijos and nietos. There are several músicos in this book who, likewise, either learned to play from their parents or were inspired by family elders.

One such individual is Cipriano Vigil, one of the most versatile and knowledgeable Hispanic musicians alive today. Cipriano, who plays a multitude of instruments, some of which he invents and fabricates himself, carries on his family tradition, playing the old songs with his father. In many ways, however, Cipriano is a unique figure. An expert on la música folklórica with an active repertoire of hundreds of songs ranging from décimas to entriegas, Cipriano is also a gifted composer of original music. He calls his work "la nueva canción nuevomexicana," identifying it with the contemporary wave of poetic, often politically inspired music in Latin America known as "la nueva canción" ("the new song"). That hemispheric link is made all the more tangible by the fact that Cipriano uses traditional Latin American instruments such as the charango in his performances.

The Chamisal native is also a crossover figure in the sense of his musical training. Like so many of his compañeros y compañeras, he began playing on his own initiative. "For as long as I can remember, ever since I was just a child, I used to go to all the bailes. But I wouldn't go to dance. No, I went to watch the músicos, to study how they played, to talk with them," Cipriano says. The learning process, he recalls, was not limited to wedding dances and Saturday night fandangos. Cipriano also remembers "la música de la resolana," gatherings on a sunny afternoon to share music along with mitote, as the vecinos taught each other the old canciones and the latest hits from the radio. Unlike those neighbors, however, Cipriano went on to seek formal musical training, attending the University of New Mexico, the University of Utah, New Mexico Highlands University, and the prestigious Instituto Nacional de Bellas Artes in Mexico City. He has produced two cassettes of folkloric and original songs, and has composed music for the stage and screen, including the film *The Milagro Beanfield War*.

Perhaps the most important work he does, however, is his teaching. Whether it's in the courses he offers at Northern New Mexico Community College or in the songs he teaches his own children to sing and perform, Cipriano is constantly working to ensure the survival of the old traditions. It's an effort that, in this age of VCR's and MTV, faces considerable odds.

Like many aspects of traditional Hispanic culture— like the Spanish language itself—the musical heritage of the Southwest is in danger of being lost in future generations. Here in Nuevo México y Viejo Colorado, the ever-loosening link with the land is, perhaps, the greatest threat to the old cultural traditions. The out-migration of families that began after World War II continues to siphon the youth away to the cities, which offer greater hope of prosperity. As Cipriano sings in the chorus of one of his compositions:

Este es el nuevomexicano
Que se encuentra por mi tierra—
Y también es un anciano
Porque el joven anda fuera.

This is the New Mexican
Who lives in this land I call my own—
He's also an elderly man
For the young ones live far from home.

Unfortunately, there is no guarantee the musical traditions will endure even among those who remain in their tierra nativa, this beautiful land which is increasingly filling up with RV's and Arby's and Sonics and satellite dishes. Every time a family hires a rock band to play for a fiftieth wedding anniversary dance, another page closes on a rich book of tradition. Every nieto who forgets the language of his ancestors or who never learned even enough Spanish to carry on a conversation with his grandmother loses a part of himself along with the music he may rarely hear and never comprehend. Every time one of the ancianos dies, part of the larger melody of the culture expires along with him or her, and the majority of músicos, it goes without saying, belong to those older generations.

In a sense, this state of affairs is nothing new. The oral

tradition—whether it be the brujerías el tío Anastacio once told by the light of the crackling fogón, or the yerbas la comadre Gorgonia used to mix as a cure for el aigre, or the old inditas about los indios de San Juan that doña Margarita liked to sing while grinding chile—the whole of the oral tradition is always on the verge of extinction. Dependent as it is on the collective memory of each successive generation, this delicate chain of words and songs and wisdom can snap at any time. That is at once the vulnerability and the great worth of the oral tradition. We value it all the more because we realize just how easily it might vanish.

There are those, of course, who have worked very hard to "rescue," if you will, elements of the oral tradition. These folklorists, historians, ethnomusicologists, and cultural anthropologists have recorded many of those precious words and fleeting tones in writing and on audio and video tape. Much of the great storytelling tradition has been preserved in print, thanks to the work of such early pioneers as Aurelio Espinoza, Américo Paredes, Aurora Lucero-White, Arthur Campa, Rubén Cobos, Lorin Brown, Reyes Martínez, Cleofas Jaramillo and, most notably, Juan B. Rael whose *Cuentos Españoles de Colorado y Nuevo México* is the prime sourcebook of the spoken story in the Hispanic Southwest. The late John D. Robb performed much the same function for Hispanic folk music, publishing the authoritative volume *Hispanic Music of New Mexico and the Southwest* and recording countless hours of music that now makes up the Robb Archive of Southwest Music at the University of New Mexico.

More recently, others have taken up the important task of recording, cataloguing, and interpreting the musical tradition, among them Cipriano Vigil, Peter White, Charles Briggs, Enrique Lamadrid, Rowena Rivera, Brenda Romero-Hymer, James Leger, and ethnomusicologist Jack Loeffler and his wife, Katherine. First on their own and later with filmmaker and photographer Jack Parsons, the Loefflers set off on a seven-year, 60,000-mile journey to find los músicos del pueblo. The result is 300,000 feet of recorded material representing some 2,000 songs, a series of 104 radio programs aired on National Public Radio, an award-winning film entitled *La Música de los Viejos,* an annual folk music festival of the same name, and now, the collection of Parsons's photographs featured in this book.

Though all of this work is invaluable, no number of transcripts or recordings—nor much less these words I write—can replace the living link, the young músico who picks up the violin and carries on the tradition. It is this vital connection between generations that is the most tenuous, for even if that joven eventually decides to learn "la raspa" along with his rock, the grandfather who might have taught him the chords will be gone.

In fact, a number of these músicos staring across time with their faces full of years had already died before this book was published. Still others are not pictured here at all, having passed away before Parsons could photograph them. Hence, the portraits of las viudas, the widows who sit alone in uncomfortable chairs, holding the snapshots of their late esposos.

But what of the hand that holds the page featuring the picture of the widow holding the picture of the músico who now only plays in her mind? Are we not in danger of ourselves becoming "cultural viudos," marooned with our memories and obsessed with a few precious images? Will we someday find ourselves in all-too-comfortable chairs, wondering how such a robust tradition could be reduced to a handful of reproductions?

Yet we love the pictures, for it is the camera lens that unites the far-flung family, magically conquering time and space to seat a long-dead bisabuelo at the glossy white edge of his great-granddaughter's First Holy Communion. Those ancestral portraits hanging over the TV are spiritual mirrors, reflecting something about ourselves that polished glass can't reveal. They give form and figure to the voices we carry in our heads—those family stories that together make up the story of a culture, those old versos and canciones that in unison create la música del pueblo.

Yesterday, while waiting in the express lane at Safeway, I was startled out of my lethargic consideration of the latest photograph of space aliens on the cover of the *Enquirer* by the sound of a voice in song. It was the young guy in the line ahead of me, singing an unconscious and exuberant rendition of "Flor de las flores." I picked up the chorus, though not quite as loudly, as I walked out to the car and realized the music can't help but go on.

PHOTOGRAPHS

Albino Gómez, singer, accordionist, Las Tablas, N.M., 1985

Abenicio Montoya, violinista, and Benny Bustos, guitarist, Santa Fe, N.M., 1983

Leandro Tórrez, violinista, singer, deceased, with Cruz Romero, guitarist, deceased,
Las Vegas, N.M., 1983

Clarence Sena, singer, Peñasco, N.M., 1986

José Martínez, guitarist, Las Vegas, N.M., 1985

Rebecca Martínez, singer, Canjilón, N.M., 1986

Archie and Maria Garduño, singers, guitarists, Las Vegas, N.M., 1986

Dennis Romero, Paul Baca, and Ronald Martínez, singers and guitarists, Canjilón, N.M., 1986

Andy, Candelaria, and Dennis Torres (and Dennis's daughter Sara), singers, guitarists, Costilla, N.M., 1987

Ventura Rael, violinista, deceased, Las Cruces, N.M., 1988

Enrique Jara, singer, guitarist, deceased, Watrous, N.M., 1984

Johnny Flórez and Raul García, singers, guitarists, Las Cruces, N.M., 1983

Jake, Juan, and Floyd Olguín, singers, guitarists, violinistas, Anton Chico, N.M., 1987

Julian Contreras, singer, guitarist, violinista, Leasburg, N.M., 1986

Margarito and Isabel War, singers, guitarists, Medenales, N.M., 1985

Emilio Ortiz, Pepe Hidalgo, and Tommy Delgadillo, singers, guitarists, Lemitar, N.M., 1983

Max Apodaca, singer, violinista, guitarist, deceased, with his wife, Antonia Apodaca,
singer and guitarist, Rociada, N.M., 1987

Mrs. Vicente Torres, accordionist, Socorro, N.M., 1986

Tony Sánchez, singer, guitarist, Clayton, N.M., 1985

Cleofas Ortiz, singer, violinista, and Augustin Chávez, guitarist, Bernal, N.M., 1988

Solomón Chavéz, singer, pianist, Alamosa, Colo., 1983

Felix Vega, guitarist, and Pete Maese, violinista, deceased, Las Cruces, N.M., 1983

Vicente Montoya, singer, violinista, deceased, and Margarito Olivas, guitarist, with his mother, Juanita Olivas, deceased, 1983

Leandro Tórrez, singer, violinista, deceased, Las Vegas, N.M., 1986

Juan Chacón, player of many instruments, San Luis, Colo., 1986

José Romero, singer, violinista, Las Vegas, N.M., 1983

Margaret Saavedra, pianist, singer, Albuquerque, N.M., 1986

Luis Martínez, violinista, Raton, N.M., 1985

Pete Chávez, guitarist, singer, his son Chris Chávez, singer, violinista, and Manuel Chávez, guitarist, Española, N.M., 1987

Cipriano Vigil, singer and player of many traditional and contemporary instruments, with his son Ciprianito, El Rito, N.M., 1988

Ruben Vigil, singer, guitarist, Albuquerque, N.M., 1986

Edwin Berry, singer, Tomé, N.M., 1983

Carmen Araiza, singer, guitarist, La Mesa, N.M., 1983

Rumaldo Guilez, harmonica player, and Concepción Guilez, singer, Tularosa, N.M.,
1986

Lorenzo and Roberto Martínez, singers and players of many instruments, including violin and guitar, Albuquerque, N.M., 1989

Claudio Saenz, singer, guitarist, La Mesa, N.M., 1986

Elias Rascón, singer, Alamosa, Colo., 1984

Isaac Chávez, singer, guitarist, Las Cruces, N.M., 1986

Edulia Romero, singer, Alamosa, Colo., 1984

Juan de la O, violinista, deceased, with his daughter, Vivian de la O, Albuquerque,
N.M., 1986

Manuel Rosas, singer, guitarist, and Roger Gabaldón, singer, Socorro, N.M., 1986

Pedro Joe Sánchez, guitarist, Clayton, N.M., 1985

Virginia Bernal, singer, guitarist, Raton, N.M., 1984

Julia Jaramillo, singer, and Ernesto Montoya, guitarist, deceased, Taos, N.M., 1983

José Archuleta, violinista, deceased, and Pablo Trujillo, guitarist, Taos, N.M., 1983

Floyd Trujillo, singer, harmonica player, Abiquiu, N.M., 1987

Roberto Mondragón, singer, guitarist, Cuyamunge, N.M., 1988

Antonio Chávez, violinista, San Juan, N.M., 1987

Sam Armijo, violinista, Gladstone, N.M., 1986

Mrs. Guadalupe Urioste, violinista, Las Vegas, N.M., 1985

Abade Martínez, singer, guitarist, harmonica player, San Luis, Colo., 1983

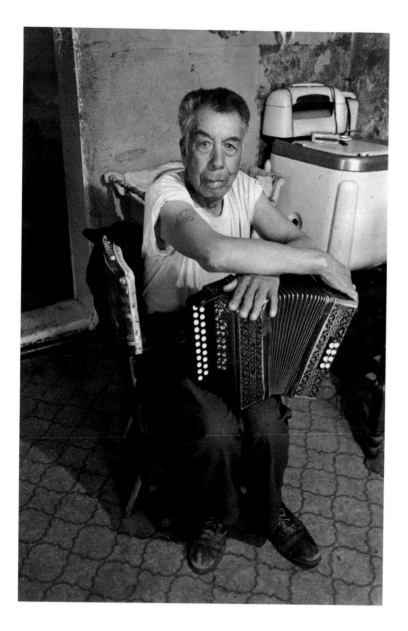

Santiago Martínez, accordionist, Las Vegas, N.M., 1983

AFTERWORD

I have now lived in southern New Mexico for twenty years and during most of that time I have been involved in taking photographs and making books and films of the cultures and lives of the people around me—Hispanic, Anglo, and Native American. I feel this has really been a gift—it has focused my work and my eye, opened me to different lives and possibilities, and given me a geography of light and landscape in which to discover myself, raise a family, and create a life.

Part of this good fortune has been the opportunity to work on many interesting projects, projects which compensated for financial loss and other negative aspects along the way in that they were my projects. This book is, obviously, such a one. In 1983 Jack Loeffler, a musician, writer, sound-recordist, and long-time collector of Hispanic folk music, and I received a grant from the National Endowment for the Arts to make a modest documentary film, *La Música de los Viejos*. This became my introduction to many of the musicians Jack and his wife Katherine had been recording. Making this film turned out to be so much fun, such pure enjoyment, that I quickly realized I wanted to continue photographing these músicos. A series of portraits seemed to be a logical conclusion; not only could I go back and photograph many of the musicians who were unable to be in the film, but I could combine this with the Hispanic music folk festivals Jack, Katherine, and I began to produce through the National Endowment for the Arts. Additionally, the Entriega project (the collecting of different musical styles and forms of traditional New Mexican entriegas) had taken shape under the guidance of Suzanne Jamison and Cipriano Vigil, allowing me further opportunities to photograph musicians in their homes throughout northern New Mexico.

In organizing the Hispanic folk music festivals, Jack and I would climb into his old Chevy truck and take off for a week at a time with a minimum of equipment—a tape recorder, a couple of cameras, and some lights—and travel the countryside visiting different musicians. While Jack would organize what they would play at the upcoming folk festival, I'd plan my photographs. After Jack was finished, I'd set up, take my pictures, and we'd be off. Without exception, the musicians were gracious and generous with their time, and there was always something in their homes to spark my eye and provide context for the portraits.

My involvement with the Entriega project was much the same. While Cipriano Vigil, Jack Loeffler and Enrique Lamadrid would record the singers of the different entriegas, I would poke around trying to find the right place for a shot. Again, there was always much to please the eye—family photographs, crocheted rugs and couch covers, old cars and trucks, a glass vase shaped like a bird, peacock feathers, an ancient refrigerator, a brightly painted wall— these homes were never boring. When I started working on these portraits I had been more intent on the musical context, but as I kept photographing, the total environment began to take over. The musicians and their environment were really such a reflection of each other it seemed incomplete to isolate either. I hope that these photographs convey some of the pleasure and delight my experience with the músicos of New Mexico and southern Colorado gave me.